A VOICE IN THE MOUNTAIN

A VOICE IN THE MOUNTAIN

POEMS BY
PETER DAVISON

ATHENEUM NEW YORK
1977

4/1978

Am. Lit

The following poems have appeared through the courtesy of magazines and newspapers, sometimes in earlier versions:

THE ATLANTIC: *The Hawk of the Mind, Hanging Man, Cross Cut, La Bocca della Verità.*
BOSTON UNIVERSITY JOURNAL: *La Cathédrale Engloutie.*
COUNTRY JOURNAL: *Haskell's Mill, Making Much of Orioles.*
GLOUCESTER TIMES: *Head Stone.*
IOWA REVIEW: *Circolo della Caccia.*
NEW REPUBLIC: *Day of Wrath.*
THE NEW YORKER: *Zenith: Walker Creek.*
POETRY NORTHWEST: *Thanksgiving, Skiing by Moonlight.*
TIMES LITERARY SUPPLEMENT (London): *The Diamond Pipe.*

*PS
3554
A94
V6*

Library of Congress Cataloging in Publication Data

Davison, Peter.
   A voice in the mountain.

   I. Title.
PS3554.A94V6   811'.5'4   77–76552
ISBN 0–689–10812–5

Copyright © 1975, 1976, 1977 by Peter Davison
All rights reserved
Published simultaneously in Canada by McClelland and Stewart Ltd
Composition by Kingsport Press, Kingsport, Tennessee
Printed and bound by Halliday Lithograph Corporation
West Hanover, Massachusetts
Designed by Harry Ford
First Edition

FOR *NATALIE WEINER DAVISON*

(1899–1959)

Für die Zeit wo du g'liebt mi hast
Dank i dir schön,
Und i wünsch, das dirs anderswo
Besser mag gehn.

And the angel of the Lord came again the second time, and touched him, and said, Arise and eat; because the journey is too great for thee.

And he arose, and did eat and drink, and went in the strength of that meat forty days and forty nights unto Horeb the mount of God.

And he came thither unto a cave, and lodged there; and, behold, the word of the Lord came to him, and he said unto him, What doest thou here, Elijah?

And he said, I have been very jealous for the Lord God of hosts: for the children of Israel have forsaken thy covenant, thrown down thine altars, and slain thy prophets with the sword; and I, even I only, am left; and they seek my life, to take it away.

And he said, Go forth, and stand upon the mount before the Lord. And, behold, the Lord passed by, and a great and strong wind rent the mountains, and brake in pieces the rocks before the Lord; but the Lord was not in the wind: and after the wind an earthquake; but the Lord was not in the earthquake:

And after the earthquake a fire; but the Lord was not in the fire: and after the fire a still small voice.

And it was so, when Elijah heard it, that he wrapped his face in his mantle, and went out, and stood in the entering in of the cave. And behold, there came a voice unto him, and said, What doest thou here, Elijah?

I KINGS: 19:7–13

CONTENTS

I   MAKING MUCH OF ORIOLES

II   THE DOLLS' HOUSE

III   THE HANGING MAN

IV *HEAD STONE*

I

MAKING MUCH OF ORIOLES

LYING IN THE SHADE   (*After Trilussa*)

Reading, as usual, in The New Yorker,
behind a haystack, chewing on a straw,
I see a swine and say, "So long, old porker!"
I see an ass and say, "So long, hee-haw!"

Such beasts won't take my meaning very far
so I'll be satisfied if I can tell
a little of the way things really are
without the risk of ending in a cell.

ALL' OMBRA (*Trilussa*)

Mentre me leggo er solito giornale
Spaparacchiato all' ombra d'un pajaro
Vedo un porco e je dico:—Addio, majale!—
Vedo un ciuccio e je dico:—Addio, somaro!—

Forse 'ste bestie nun me capiranno,
Ma provo armeno la soddisfazione
De poté dí le cose come stanno
Senza paura de finí in priggione.

CIRCOLO DELLA CACCIA

For Douglas Allanbrook

Italian butchers love the shooting season.
It lasts at least six months, some places longer.
Thrushes, larks, and other speckled singers
hang up to ripen, dangling by their bloody
beaks, eyes glassy, feather coats bedraggled.
Any old bird who makes it through the season
has lasted out a war—the hunters number
twice any army Italy has mustered—
imposing laws of natural selection
for songlessness or silence in the woods.
Just scuff your shoe on any gravel walk
and thickets are vacated on the instant
with a desperate scramble and a chirped alarm.
Then hours go by without a glimpse of a bird,
just distant songs of sex and altercations.
You wonder why the hunters never shoot
at swallows that patrol the city rivers
hell-bent as bats, or bag the swifts that twitter
above your head at cocktails on the terrace.
Though songbirds of open spaces, fields and mountains
are hunted down, fair game, to turn on spits
and freshen the mouth's appetite for wine,
I once for three acts watched a sparrow flutter
around an opera house's chandelier
while every eye was fixed upon Mimi
and no one noticed the bird until he dropped
dead on the stage abaft of the soprano.

ZENITH: WALKER CREEK

The woodcock now spends his evenings more quietly.
The robin sings less urgently, more chirpy.
Grass which sprang up for a while as though
it meant to reach the stars each afternoon
has moderated its ambitions a little.
The fields have settled down to heavy feeding and breeding.
Marsh, its winter khaki conquered,
has greened itself into equator color,
swaying taller and taller with the tides' tickling.
"Nature's first green is gold." Her second
is opaque as billiard tables. Now she plays her game,
less urgency in the dawns, less melodrama.
The pheasant's declaration rings out half as often;
the minnows flutter calmly in their pools,
having learned their prey cannot escape.
The shade is deeper, more desirable.
Dogs trot in preference to running,
spend more of daylight sprawling and panting.
The pedalling bicyclists shift to lower gears,
the bay blooms with looser and larger sails.
Our sun has given of its best in waxing:
It teeters above our heads as nearly
as the earth's escapism will permit,
toppling with some reluctance after noon
toward the West to keep us on the boil
till the anger of flies and the hunger of mosquitoes
drive us from sun to shade, from shade to the shelter
of screens, where, after fall of darkness, we drown
our senses in sunburn, poison ivy, gin.
Drinking deep, hot-headed, we sleep dark.
Those long days were the promises we broke.

BICENTENNIAL

The cinquefoil in the field
stands up to yellow clover,
strawberries, hawkweed,
daisies almost now over.

Swallows dive and swoop;
they tremble, glide and roll.
Necklaces of wren-song
chatter down the stone wall.

Roses stud the edge of the woods
where goldenrod is growing.
Ovenbirds are teaching.
Cattle might be lowing

were trees not making motions
to wipe our fields away.
Two hundred years of farming?
A single stand of hay.

MAKING MUCH OF ORIOLES

Teetering high in the feathers of an elm,
two orioles chortled halfway into spring
while their green cover faded into dun
breasting the normal current of the season.
The tree trunk bled wet life into the ground.
Dutch elm disease. The tree had been no beauty,
strangled in its early days by grapevine,
embraced by poison ivy, tickled by thistles;
yet when it was felled an unfamiliar light
erased familiar shadows from the garden.

I walked around the tree to count the branches
that must be lopped before the trunk could be
bucked into cordwood. Here, suspended sideways
a pouch of gray silk dangled, gave out peeping.
Three chicks inside, as featherless and bright
as oranges, crouched back and yawned in my face.
Parental discord rang from the nearby willows.

Maybe the nest could be removed, like houses
that block the highway, crawling on a trailer,
or bob behind a tugboat, buoyed and hawsered
betwixt the fishing villages of Newfoundland.
I pruned the dangling branch that held the nest
at its tip, like moss wrapped round a finger,
and cradled it along a ladder, stretched
as high up a chokecherry tree as I could reach,
fifty feet short of normal oriole altitude.
The chicks kept cheeping, fearful for their balance
when borne by clumsy hands and not the wind.
With every knot I wound another tie
between the elm branch and the cherry tree
hanging the nest too high for predators.

Now for the parents, fixated on elms.
They hovered frantically near the supine tree
in search of the family they'd left dangling,
three chicks too small to fly, a nest
redoubtable enough to brave the elements.
How to believe that house could simply vanish
to rebuild in an unfamiliar tree?
I waited, sometimes whistling their calls,
a mocking-man who sang in dialect.
It might—or not—have been an accident
that before sundown the elders took their nest
at cherry value, unfamiliar height,
with chicks inside that must have been their own.
For several weeks I watched them come and go,
mother or father fetching food, while one
sang unto heaven in a higher tree.
The elm-leaves grew brown and dry and dead,
but twine still bound elm to the darker cherry
while, in the nest, the chicks gained flying weight.

One morning in July the nest was empty.
The younger and the older birds had gone:
parents and children roamed the world together.
The withered nest hung on, now limp, a trophy
of something like a victory of will.
I climbed the ladder to untie my knots
and hung the dried branch with its tattered flag
on the wall of my room, perhaps to hatch its meaning.

But a nest is no place to arrest a song
that in its very nature has no end.
The second year the orioles found an elm
to build in somewhere in the neighborhood.
They might have been my nestlings. I don't know.
I've tossed the branch behind a lilac bush.

DAY OF WRATH

September silence sags over the field.
Faded summer denims flap with fatigue
on a neighbor's clothesline.
No birds sing, only crickets and katydids.
Yesterday the heaven twittered with swallows;
today at noon the wires are swept empty
of occupants. From an enormous distance
the crow cries out his carrion comfort.
The pasture, lately mowed, noses aside yellow bristles
with a new cropspill of bluegreen autumn blades.
The sun sizzles on rocks, striking raisinly wrinkles
into the unpicked grapes, which white-tailed hornets
ignore, to feast on the drowsy flies
who do not hear them coming.
The marsh tides move like syrup.
Their dark water stirs the seed-heavy grasses
like masts of sloops at anchor.
Beechnut hulls bristle under the
toughening hats of their leafage.
Gardens have been harvested of beans and corn.
The dry soil flourishes mostly with immigrants:
brussels sprouts, broccoli, *aubergines, poireaux.*
Shortening days turn crisp after nightfall.
By day the air still hums with the sound of sleep.
This afternoon is tangled in its silence
until a yellow dog, posted to guard an empty house,
lets out a howl. His desertedness will never end.
No man will cross the road for his relief.
His work of watching will go on forever.

AUTUMN ZODIAC

For J. B. Priestley at Eighty

I   SEEDTIME

Born at the edge of a century, just between seasons
under the sign of Virgo, no springtime spirit,
your colors mingle into autumn gold.
With veteran zest, as one who trudged more leagues
and could empty more tankards than others would attempt,
you laid about you in youth, crested, rumbustious,
and drubbing the heads of the dons; your lower lip jutted
in not-to-be-feigned disrespect—oh, how you had at them!

Rampant and headstrong as Merino rams
whose fleece you tallied for a Bradford merchant,
you clattered aslant the ordered lines of language
in waves of words to heal the wartime wounds
and keep their silence—hardly a mention of battle
in all the rest of your years after the terrible war.
Later, pierced with knowledge that death could edge
across your path in costumes other than khaki,
you put your pain to work like one possessed:
survival kept your mind alive as your body.
Joy bloomed from grief in dark, unlikely weather:
Mr. Smeeth walked in majesty over the mountains of Brahms.

Autumn houses her faith in dreams of spring:
her toughened dusky petals hold till frost
the cells of sprigs that woke along the marl
before a mote of color starred the garden.
September roses keep their youth alive
till all the jonquils' fingerholds have sunk
deep into memory: could they have ever existed?

You often tease us into springtime dreams
of all the bright days that preceded this one,
such memories as time has laid to sleep,
roles in the play we all perform together,
seasons never forgotten though forgotten.
The years swim forward in your scenes and pages
to the dressing-room where each, wherever his seat,
must stare at the unfamiliar face of his mirror.
There the cold caustic of our century
has scarred the promises that we believed.
Yet Virgo smiles at us like every wife
who owes her harvest to unclouded spring.

CROSS CUT

Slumped on a pallet of winter-withered grass
you lie dead at my feet, in age not quite
a century, perhaps, but twice as old as I am,
in a pose your twisted trunk and dwindling leaves
had never hinted, even at your sickest.
How many stubs your gangrened upper branches
had turned into sockets and armpits
for squirrel, coon and starling
to burrow in! You thrust erect as stiff
as the memory of my oldest neighbor who watches
each new spring for your fluttering bloom
and every August for a pride of pears—
green to the eye, woody to the tooth,
taut and cidery to the fumbling tongue.
For years we've watched you dying from the top,
a peril to climbing children and seekers of shade,
but knew that, pear-like, you could stand for years,
heart eaten out, just fingering your life.
Perhaps I could have helped you out of the air
with some shreds of your stature left intact,
but now I've failed you. You lie invisible
behind the wall, your most disgraceful branches
lopped and hauled for firewood, resting scarred,
beyond your element, crushed by your own weight,
shapeless and pitiful as a beachbound whale.
Only inches above the nourishing ground
a cross-cut stump, stark white, reveals at bottom
you're still as lively as the day you bloomed.
The hearts of your leaves shone out in valentines
and your windborne, lilting, sinewy boughs
heaped proudly up toward the waning sun
those glowing, softly tinted, bumper bushels.

SKIING BY MOONLIGHT

Orion reclines on his hip.
Polaris glares high at my left.
I glide my way homeward
a quarter-moon chasing me.

We follow the lurching shadow
of my sweaty body back
along the newly-crumbled tracks
I slogged only an hour ago

through the mirror-image pasture.
(Polaris twinkled at my right,
Orion teetered at my left;
the moon, narrow as a candle,

sparkled on smooth, blameless snow,
a beach of diamonds.
Cedars were heaped with treasure
among frozen cherry trees.)

Our sheep have all taken shelter
within the black barn.
In the windless moonlight
only an owl hoots against the cold

while deer, silent among pines,
wait to hear my skis stop hissing
and the back door click shut

before they wade toward the rick
to steal some hay.

THE HAWK OF THE MIND

No mind, no mind. What settles down around me
must not be left for the rain to wash away.
I need my mind, but no, it will not answer.
The maples are darkening in the August day.
The standing grass is drying into hay.
Swallows, fledged and grown, chatter in the sky
or warm themselves on the rooftree.
Their blood has not yet been spilled,
but the hawk of the mind is waiting.

HASKELL'S MILL

For Percy Roberts, late of West Gloucester

The breeze wheels westerly and puffs a net
that hangs between two branches. There's a hammer
driving new nails into the barn's new shingles.
Yet also far away I hear the hammer
that crushes city buildings into rubble,
demolishes the landmarks of a nation
beneath the spiderweb of Brooklyn Bridge.
Hard by the seaside, on a farm, an island
that looks both landward and toward the tides
and hears surf hammering beyond the hill,
tales are told of a mill, long since abandoned,
that cooled the heels of a hundred Union soldiers
sweating in bivouac on a summer day.
("Their captain marched them down to the creek
at high tide and off the mill dam, in columns.")
It stood within eyeshot of this farmhouse,
yet not for ninety years has Haskell's Mill
ground a single particle of grain.

Without the power harnessed in the waters
a mill's no more than an abandoned city,
a legend in the landscape, a location
without an edifice or an inhabitant,
only a name beside the reckless tides,
the water's roar, the grinding of the stones.
The city grows, a cancer between rivers.
The outposts on the islands are deserted.
Our farms are farmland only in the deed
and finally revert to wilderness
because no one of us has got the heart
to keep his hopes alive. Sumac, black cherry

throw sprouts around the rocks that once were bared
by sheep that grazed at large in open pastures
until the dogs grew bold and ran them off.
My neighbors breed, and spin their wheels, and hold
their land in hopes developers will buy
to spare them the indignity of ruins.
Their houses fill up with wornout machines
and in their woodlots cars are left for dead,
oozing a smell of gasoline and rubber
consumed to make a city of the country
where nothing is produced and little earned.

Not far along the creek lies what is left
of Haskell's Mill: "The remains of the dam, some rocks
and waterlogged timbers." The Haskells had been given
"the licence of the town in 1690
to build this tide mill for grinding corn.
The tide was high enough there, certainly,
to make a pool of every incoming tide . . .
The controlled outflow turned the water wheel . . .
Vessels are claimed to have docked here
to take on meal for the West Indies trade." *
Beside the creek, where boys still dig for worms,
the spot that once was known for Haskell's Mill
lies unremarked across the salt-hay marshes.
A ruined skiff rots by the waterside.
The yellowlegs and plover scream in voices
anxious with autumn, with migration coming.
High tide pours in, kingfishers skim the pool,
crabs nibble at the rising of the tide,
and gulls search hopefully along the brink,
take flight for higher ground till the tide turns.

* Joseph E. Garland, *The Gloucester Guide*, 1973

I stand where men made something of the earth.
Dependent on the soil, the moon, the sea
whose surf is muttering behind the dunes,
they planted corn and ground it into meal
without the use of any other force
than nature's, than the mind's. Down a short track
the shingled house of food stood by the water.
Inside, a rope, the thickness of an arm,
held heavy millstones, grooved and geared to grind
opposed, in and out of disengagement,
governed by pulleys and levers with wooden handles
to make the slab stones kiss and scour each other.
At every touch white flour puffed and drizzled
down through a funnel in the nether millstone
to rise like bleached sand in an hourglass
until the hopper filled, and then the mealsacks,
and then the lighters waiting for the ships
to weigh anchor and set sail for the islands.

In spring above the creek the first strong thrust
of green is of asparagus, large-leaved rhubarb;
next mushrooms red and white, sorrel, sourgrass,
lettuce in the garden, sage and radishes.
In other times cows cropped the early grass
and piglets scuffled trotters in the rain
that dripped from the eaves of the unloaded barn,
while apple and pear trees gasped into blossom.
Later came blackberries, gooseberries, currants,
eggplant and beans, basil, fennel, onions,
and all the rambling plenitude of squash—
food in the places where there were no woods,
in open places, corn and wheat for meal.

Two millstones now lie buried in the ground,
doorsteps to the houses of two neighbors
unborn the day the stones crushed their last kernel
and creaked into disuse, desertion, silence.
The tide now scrapes and rattles fists of stone
at random. Men withdraw allegiance
from land and sea. They take their pay from strangers.
After two hundred years while Haskell's Mill
tugged wagons full of corn to the waterside,
men spilled the stones their fathers linked together
to make the tides perform a human service:
to feed themselves by the inanimate.
Enlarging peasant patience with the craft
of millers, moving stones by water,
men turned mere fodder into manly meal
enough to feed the outcasts of the islands.
The girded miller, prostitute and priest,
served in an apron crusted stiff with flour
while water roared and millwheels groaned near by.
He summoned the fruits of the earth to the shore of the sea.
He kept the balance between life and death,
the sun and moon, the water and the stone.

THANKSGIVING

For Gunilla Jainchill

By the authority vested in me, a gift,
(in German, *poison;* in Swedish, *a marriage*)
I write of journeys, landscapes, interventions,
inheritances visible, alive, or dead.
A milkweed pod atop its autumn stalk
bulges from cold and flips itself wide open.
It sprinkles flurries of snow among the grass
to bloom, mulberry-like, for next midsummer,
nourished by milk no bitterer, no whiter
than any I have tasted as a gift.

II

THE DOLLS' HOUSE

THE FALL OF THE DOLLS' HOUSE

The family figurines sat round a fire
at the hearth of a dolls' house, porcelain-faced,
dove-breasted, leaning against each other.
They smiled as though their rage were ruled by music,
the transcendental chords of Plato's dream.
Father, a kindly provider, judge, and priest.
Mother, a milkmaid, mending things and healing.
Children at play, at rest, reading their lessons—
such are the lessons that our lessons taught.
A window-frame hemmed in this perfect scene
for all to worship, as we worship icons.

Beside the dolls' house that the family built
the father's drunk. His wife weeps for her sex.
Young Tim is crippled and will surely die.
The older children dream of rape and murder,
for which of them has strength enough to act
as ancestor? The dolls' house shows them how
all parents fail, the Virgin fails the Child.
Their icon topples before war, change, chaos;
embraces yield to riot in the streets.
The pulse beats hard when Manson or Attila
kicks in the fire door, wrestles down Papá,
mugs mother, rapes the girl, snaps like twigs
the GI crutches of poor Tiny Tim.

Look at the dolls' house my grandparents owned,
its furniture imported from Saxe-Coburg,
in this contented photo. In another
the harmony of Diderot and Newton
takes on the dissonance of Marx and Freud.
My parents' glamor hints a naughty streak:
these dolls wear knickers, camisoles, bandeaux.

23

In a more recent snap, my wife and I,
nurtured on Tillich, Kierkegaard, and Jung,
wear casual clothes but strike a mannered pose.
I slouch eccentric, while she smiles, protecting
the children underneath a cherry tree.
We'll leave the house, I think. The leaves are falling.

My children see themselves as in a poster:
unisex, well-provided, amplified.
Shatter the house, my darlings, helter-skelter.
The harmonies of our philosophy
have let us sleep through years of cuckoo-clocks
in drawing-rooms of matchsticks, cards, and lace.
If you are granted wishes for the world,
enlarge its scope: make work as one with play
in houses built for everlasting fire
where man and woman burn like seraphim.

OFFISSA POPP

A Maneuver in Class Warfare

My father suited up
for two world wars
but was never recruited
to clean a weapon:
officer material.
Between wars he fancied
firing a borrowed shotgun
at (or near) birds.
But once a pheasant
whom he had stunned
and left me to carry
came undone.
Father strode on
gunning and missing.
His bird woke up
and stared me down.
The two of us sat
in the stubbled cornfield.
That was that.

One war later
he took up skeet.
His pals at the range
kept his twelve-gauge shiny;
but when he made
his big move to town
the gun was cleaned,
packed up, broke down.

A third war came
along, and I
went off to do
my hitch—G.I.
On my discharge
my father pleaded
he badly needed
his shotgun cleaned.
He needed it now
but he didn't know how.
As a boy whose mother
had never let him bother
with guns or other
store-bought mayhem,
I wondered why
a former G.I.
should serve this two-time fat man
as a batman?

Duty scoured the Winchester
with patches and rods.
Apologizing to the gods
of war, I poured,
and smeared the pad
with olive oil
(nothing else on hand)
and scrubbed out the gun
in pride and pity,
preserving the citi-
zens' right to bear
arms, by hiding a piece
like an adulterer's underwear
behind the galoshes
in a sixteenth-floor closet
on Fifty-seventh Street
in New York City.

Oh I polished the gun
he thought he might flourish
but he never assembled it
before he passed on.
When his executor
sold it for a pittance,
it was lubricated all right.
The bore shone bright.
An enlisted man's fate
is to clean his gun
before he may eat.
I should have beat-
en the thing into
a goddam plowshare.

MEMOIR:
"What thou lov'st well shall not be reft from thee"

A child may swell himself into a hero,
an Oedipus among his generation,
choking the bed where he was made.
Pretend that you have really "been adopted,"
that those who nurtured you were shepherds.
Indulge a disposition to scatter love.
Stir up expectations past redeeming.
Thighs part. Sex dreams its way to bloom.
You're free to love, you tell yourself in youth,
though every kiss arouses bitter questions
and your hunger squeezes groans from the sweet feeders.

The very bodies that our bodies worshipped
loomed round the childhood table, gesturing
in kindness, anger, laughter, sobs and joy.
How could a child be free of choosing
if every kiss aroused its bitter question,
kisses of incest or adultery?
With every kiss the prince must pay a price
whether in metamorphosis or by ordeal.

The seedling sprouts, puts out unlikely flowers.
We forecast gold, the dahlias bloom in rust.
Hunger gives pain and must be fed. Kisses
turn into punishments, into rewards.
The world about the house becomes entangled
with vines that choke it, bridges that wash out,
walls to be mended, crops to weed and reap.
The growth is rank, unpredictable.
Rise from your garden, dust your callused hands
with caution for the stiffened back,
and walk in middle age toward a house.

If love be planted deep, it passeth Time.
Such love, such houses are best served by gardens
that have no bodies buried at the root
for fertilizing secrets or remorse.
We never shall be free of what we choose.
Choose then: choose houses, gardens, freedom.

THE GENIE IN THE BOTTLE

Keats and Emily D. alone of poets—
since the French revolution Blake approved of—
were mostly blighted in love:
there is evidence of syphilis even here.
Others, most others, love widely, unwisely.
Some are deluded
that being loved is what will make them great.
Monogamy gives poets very little
except for their Victorian good name.
John Berryman observes, in LOVE & FAME,
the strict construction of those two desires;
and who has got a better metaphor
than an old American poet imprisoned
in an Italian villa with two wives? AOI.

Two of our titans, born Victorians,
held themselves aloof from being touched
or being brushed by moths that singe
frail wings upon the wicks of poetry.
Frost, killingly monogamous, gossiped
with relish about his brother-poets' sins
but hardly mentioned sex in all his work.
Hardy, who made the cosmos weep for the loss of love
"fell in love" at every street corner.
Poets would seem to be susceptible.

When someone asked old Doc Williams
if he'd ever laid eyes upon a woman
he didn't care to sleep with, he
barked back, "Hell, no."

HOUSE HOLDING

For Carleton Coon and Peter Blake, who have never met.

> *Except the Lord build the house, they labor in*
> *vain that build it; except the Lord keep the city, the*
> *watchman waketh but in vain.*
> *It is vain for you to rise up early, to sit up late,*
> *to eat the bread of sorrows; for so He giveth his be-*
> *loved sleep.*   PSALM 127

BEFORE HOUSES

Hunters kept fire and (sometimes) dogs in common.
They travelled light, only tools and clothes,
built lean-tos on boreal hunting-grounds
or by the shores of salmon-sweetened rivers.
What Mother Forest offered they shared out
in portions that the gods had pre-ordained
and only shamans dared to violate.
When they moved on to gentler hunting-grounds
they hung a gift from a branch to placate spirits.

SINCE BETHLEHEM

The Holy Family might have lived today:
no resident father, invisible means of support,
mother under age. Son takes to the road
denouncing the mother, denying earthly parents,
enlisting a gang of his contemporaries
for super-societal imperatives.
This family history nearly crushed the West:
for many centuries we heard far less
of where men lived than where they worshipped.

31

What towns we had grew up around the temples,
basilicas, cathedrals. The lord's keep thickened
into a fortress under liege protection.
A villein's hut gave pairs of bodies a place
to come together nameless and start again.

THE NEW WORLD

They came to America to seek their "fortune"
(in other words, some land to build a house).
As immigrants they always talked of *home*,
called themselves *homebodies*, *homeward bound*,
were verbed by houses—*housed*, *housebound*, *housewarming*.
Thoreau, most virginal of men, inveighed
at snails weighed down by barns upon their backs.
Strip off, he said, and take yourselves to the woods.
The woods grew gloomy with disfranchised men
whose barns sagged down on them and wives despaired,
their children stunted. Cattle died. Game
grew scarce in field and woodland. Backyards
filled up with crippled and corroding Plymouths.
They shut the house and looked for work in the city.
Their sons went off in wartime to defend
whatever everyone had meant by *home*.
On upland acres, toppling granite walls
wander forgotten through a maple forest
to disappear in beaver-ponds and swamp.
Clearings crowd in upon old cellar-holes
marked by a lilac clump or rambler rose.
The country, though it emptied into town,
kept hold upon the brave, the poor, the haunted.
Transplanted sons bought up abandoned farms
to travel miles and miles to reach a house
they'd use to rest their bodies from the journey.

Overgrown hayfields and logging roads
have been spruced up with knotty-pine chalets
built *pour le sport* and locked up out of season.
Wild snowmobiles arrive on winter nights
to howl an hour or so, leave a window smashed,
allowing birds and beasts to enter in
and breed a second generation of ruin.

HOUSING STARTS

Most animals have no houses, only holes
to sleep and breed and shut things out. Held in
on themselves by scales, shells, feathers, fur,
reflexes, instinct, most of all a surer
sense of their senses, bodies are their houses.
Man's models for the house are nests and keeps.
(Most women tend to think of it as nest.)
A house has "many mansions." It is built
on sand or on a rock. A house is haunted.
A child thinks of his house as being his
before he thinks of land as being his.
Sometimes the house is make of cake. Sometimes
it's a high castle with a hedge of thorns,
or else a cosy cottage in the woods
with milk and strawberries on a wooden table.

ELEVATIONS

As citizens we seal ourselves in cells.
Thanks to our furnaces, pumps and wires,
each family has its fixtures. Even dogs
have private kennels, which their masters share.
When tenants meet in halls or elevators
they have no space or leisure to display

whether they're bent on hunger or on war.
They offer grins that are uneasy mixtures.
Each Living Unit stands upon the walls
of one beneath, shouldering one above.
Those who have no names, who share a wall with us,
we hear them and we hate them all. We know
six families live their lives beneath our carpet
(six more beneath our neighbor's and his neighbor's).
We have collected into humming hives
chiefly for profit. Nothing is collective
but passages for entry or for voiding.
Each couple makes its bed within a cube
to make of it a poem or a grave—
or just enough of each to found a family.

THE RADIANT CITY

Thus with concrete and steel new men
have taught us to employ clean catalogues
to plan our houses. Public law defends
their right to build, a right we have disused
along with other arts we have forgotten.
We camp outside until the men have finished,
and only then move in and leave the women
to settle our prefabricated chairs
and pets and pictures. Men make easy exits.
They leave their charming women to endure
in men-built houses, in their mastered lives.
Once they have settled in the frightened suburb,
wives dedicate their houses to the night,
absent themselves by day. Till recently
they had not known escape unless by force
or poverty, to factories or mines,
theatres or brothels, likely marriages.
Now they move boldly, yearn to be more manly.

34

STRICT CONSTRUCTION

In high-rise offices the males agree
that our republic's democratic creed
requires a house for feeding in and sleeping.
"New housing is a crying social need."
Men assume positions where they can
cover with walls their women's nakedness
and rear in children visions for a man.
Housing in quantity expels distress.
Why then, returning home at night, do we
find women cursing and our children weeping?

LA CATHÉDRALE ENGLOUTIE

An ancient place. The roofs are high and grey.
A friend and I walk down a cobbled street.
I've never seen an alleyway so neat:
brisk brooms have swept each speck of dust away.

No motor, tire or wheel makes hiss or clatter
across the squares or past the whitewashed angles.
My friend says, "Poor and rich agree: no wrangles!
Here nothing has ever seemed to be the matter."

In the cathedral square the Church stands fast:
its leaded panes of red and blue depict
a squad of sturdy saints, with spires erect
unsmirched by soot or by iconoclast.

Within, black hats and furled umbrellas press
past chapels of mahogany, toward cages
that stand behind the apse, to bank their wages
and scribble checks where sinners could confess.

Observe the great south aisle, the Bishop's Tomb:
walk out into the nave. No monk or priest
makes antiphon, and no one kneels. From east
to west a flock of tables fills the room,

and banqueters participate in revel.
They dance and drink from foamy steins of beer
between the speeches. How they love to hear
that cash has saved the country from the devil!

"Listen, my friend, what made your family chafe
to live in any other town? Why here?"
We walk in silence through another square.
"The schools are good," he sighs. "The streets are safe."

III

THE HANGING MAN

THE HANGING MAN

Hoist by an ankle,
my every joint squeaks.
Hair hangs from my head
as though scared to death.
I am held to the globe
by anti-gravity.
Pigs and chickens, however,
stroll past on the ceiling
apparently none the worse.

One gets used to anything.
Water runs uphill,
clouds rub their backs on the floor,
sunshine leaks its way
up through a hole in the ground.
Despite my excitable hair
I look introverted
(so upright friends tell me):
an arm and leg akimbo,
the ankle below the right foot
structurally startling.

A world like this
(Was there another?)
sets me tip-top,
hangdog, invert,
slewfoot, periculous.
I sway with each breeze
that whistles past my foot
and peep at overhead pebbles
whirling like hail;

but I see what the pigs
and chickens cannot see:
a world running down
despite all appearances.
Tolerating this anti-world
has made me the only
joke in the deck.
My only hope
is to be dealt with
or cut down.

JESUS SHAVES

In this glass what fleshly features
glance at lather, squint at blade,
at a half-awakened creature's
face unshaven, fate half-made?

Now he strops and next he barbers
what he grew as a disguise:
hair and beard, mock-mask that harbors
each expressive enterprise

he, as Leader, must engage in.
What mere mirror's glass can frame
grimaces his face will age in?
Deeds must win this face a name.

In the cavern where the dove
dropped the seed and closed the ring,
sacred, faceless, dark with love,
God endowed this naked thing.

GRATIFIED DESIRES

All unusual energy is inspired by
an unusual degree of vanity.

For my part I would rather be
mad with truth than sane with lies.

FROM *The Autobiography of*
Bertrand Russell

The Wrangler saddled myriads of words
to prove his truth was Truth, our lies were lies.
With symbols, logic, omens from the birds,
he sorted geese from swans and fools from wise.

Passion he knew, or noticed in the mirror.
With wit he braced and scandalized the schools.
Never too modest to compound an error
his lash laid wickedness on still more fools.

Reason exhausted him at thirty-five.
He'd cracked the mainspring of a storied mind
with sixty years still left to stay alive
and cleanse himself with efforts to be kind.

Famous with reason, all the world his stage,
but half its actors masked, unheard, unwed,
he made his foes his friends, his youth his age,
and anger harnessed reason by the head.

Love ruled his heart. It pierced him to the core
each time it pounced and took him by surprise
or left him faithless, naked on the shore
whenever Eros ceased to tyrannize.

At last geese claim him for the cause of Right
to prop before a crowd or sign a letter
veiling in hate the sentences of light.
My noble lord, you might have ended better.

LAMIA

The times have not been good to you, my dear,
winds blowing cold when you were trembling hot,
a climate feeding what you hadn't got.
You feared that you had even more to fear.
Striving for name and fame and such small beer
you steeped your loathed body in a pot
of remedies, experiment or not,
hearing what healers wanted you to hear.
Your eyes, puffed up with shades of pity, saw
in other faces a surreal reflection,
a row of grinning bottles on a shelf.
Entrapped, you'd leave a hand, a gnawed-off paw,
would welcome death in favor of rejection
from the one ghost who speaks for you yourself.

THE COMPOUND EYE

For L. E. Sissman, 1928–1976

What an intolerable deal of history!
You were the fly upon a thousand walls,
the poet's eye with many hundred lenses,
master of every curiosity.
Marked down for death, nipped early at the heels,
you walked with shambling evasion, not in a hurry,
too proud to betray the merest smudge of panic.
Yet in your poems death lies never far
from the surface, knife beneath the water,
dark age pending. To stay alive for it
tubers and relics of each season's growth
must be tucked into order, time, and place.
Familiar phrases bowed beneath strange burdens
("a pleasure dome of Klees and Watteaus made"),
pleasures of a couplet coupled with
the nausea of chemotherapy.
Amid the disorder of illness, dying, death,
you put in order your arrested life.

Go, prince: peer owlish through the windowpane
betwixt the daintiness of your imagination
and all the tawdriness and disarray
our life is dressed in. From the postwar city
look out at the city of God, and then confess
how sweet was the disorder in the dress.

TOWARD AN UNDERSTANDING OF
THE PUBLIC LIFE

The President, my father, and myself
drove out along Route 6. Dog came for the ride.
The President had just resigned. Father was some years dead.
The President was clearly loth
to attract public notice. No one in the car
except for Dog had much to say to Nixon,
but otherwise we travelled pretty easy.
In mid-Cape Cod a tire blew out. The President was amazed, for in High Office such
things hardly ever happen. He refused to dismount.
Nothing for me but to hoof it, lugging a three-gallon can.
I found no filling-stations open (the roads
were crowded with traffic attending Gaudí cathedrals)
but I did locate a garage, sited where two one-way
streets began: where cars might leave but not enter.
Our options exhausted, we abandoned the car
and checked ourselves into a small hotel
where tongue-and-groove planks line the corridor,
floors dark with rust-and-green linoleum.
Here we lodge to this day: my father dead and silent,
Dog an unregistered guest. I observe
and record the President's words. He paces his room
insisting on his innocence and our guilt.

RIVER BED

Where in the world
have I hidden the self you gave me?
Morning after morning I lose
my appetite for what will keep you alive.
I have forgotten
what I prayed not to forget,
the oath to myself.

I have climbed back up country
with a hazel wand
split like a woman
dowsing for tributaries
to lead me to sources:
but I am weakened by falls,
washed back past rapids, over sandbars,
through alluvial valleys
and the pollution of cities.
My body wallows through
intricate meanders
as though travelling
toward the ultimate delta.
Brackish water carries me down, down
through the frozen land of the present
farther than ever
from the springs of the crystal past
toward the finite
risks of the sea.

The waterlogged corpse
surfaces, beckoning.
His sightlessness widens my eyes.
I walk erect,
landed, dry, free.

He lifts the hard hod from my shoulders.
My head is empty of the war.
At last, without budging,
pointing my ears forward,
I hear again the forgotten
song of myself.

THE POEM IN THE PARK

She waited eagerly on a park bench,
holding in her arms the humming of the day,
her eyes welling with *lacrimae rerum*.
I walked toward her through the bricky streets
tasting as I came the sky of the public park,
its gates ajar, its paths cast wide in welcome,
the bench warm beside her
with the words the poem and I would engage together.
But as I walked in under the sighing trees,
a gust of wind scattered from the dark pond
a flock of mallards, wings whistling,
crying out and fanning toward the harbor
over the buildings between the park and the sea.

Not till hours later, hemmed in between
office telephone and office typewriter,
did it come back to me. I'd left the poem
seated motionless upon a wooden bench
with tears in its eyes.

IV

HEAD STONE

THE DIAMOND PIPE

For Dan Jacobson

Fumbled out of the earth
by what sluices and clay-clotted fingers,
plucked under the stern-eyed faces
of inspectors and watchmen,
breathlessly guarded, sorted, parcelled out
in walled and fanged secrecy
among cramped artisans for cutting and polishing,
this heap, this sandpile, this burnished pipe
of jewels lie, scatterlights,
facet and mirrored subfacet, lurking inside the dark hall
while alarms and chains hold back the surge of the crowd.

Opening time. The greatest show on earth,
the most sublime ingathering of light,
the most singular collection of the most
precious stones from the largest
diamond pipe ever tapped,
draws queues and columns of gawkers
to line the block in ranks while the cars
of millionaires draw to the curb
for the opening. The lights are about to go on.
Resting upon their cushions of black and scarlet velvet,
the gems have done their work, completed their
struggle for survival, finished their vegetable thrust
toward the light. Water, food, fertilization were all
accomplished millions of years ago.
They of all living things are the survivors.
They lie in the dark in silence
awaiting adoration.

LA BOCCA DELLA VERITÀ

> . . . *One of those pleasant old watercolors of Rome . . . the little piazza called the Mouth of Truth after the big marble face of the sun in the church portico, whose mouth was supposed to snap shut if you put your hand in it and told a lie, but which was perhaps an ancient sewer lid . . .*
>
> ELEANOR CLARK, *Rome and a Villa*

I thrust my fingers, crossed in an artful lie,
into the mouth of truth, the fluid of sex,
the darkness of death, murmuring tuneful noises.
The porch of a church ought to be good for a gamble.
In front, the face of the sun. Behind, the temples,
one round, the Temple of Vesta, home and hearth,
one square, the Temple della Fortuna Virile.
Both sexes call on us to tell the truth.

If I speak out, will doves and bluebirds descend
and the butterflies of the world slip their leashes?
If I tell, will tigers carry me to Tibet
or elect me poet-priest of a sunlit island?
I have turned away from the pleaders
and pretended to be asleep.
Only a stone's throw from Cloaca Maxima
I cringe in the lap of the great goddess,
shrinking from these monumental Roman exertions.
Who asked my soul to magnify the Lord?

Take the right hand. Place it in the sun's mouth.
If art is not "a lie that tells the truth,"
why else, except in aid of some good god,
should I hope to tell the world my kind of lie
and not be swallowed by a river of darkness?

I dare to pledge my powers to the sun.
How coldly will the marble give its answer?
If I have truly lied in the mouth of truth
let my right hand forget her cunning.

HEAD STONE

The great rock blazes high above the marsh.
From its highest foothold my father's ashes were scattered.
Much lordlier than any human chieftain,
the cliff allows high tides to lick its foot
and gathers pines around it like a blanket.
When I'm asleep, as well be dead as absent
from weather and the rock. The trees, unpruned,
squeeze out new shoots despite all seasons' endings.
The compost seethes beneath its quilt of straw.
In the autumn, sun springs up in the grass but freezes,
halted by dark winds jostling from the mountains
to kindle maple, sumac, beech and oak
into cold standards gorged erect with flame.
The land is all I'm given to imagine.
In absences I might as well be dead,
a vole's trig corpse beneath the currant bushes.
What goes on, gone? Friends die. Some few of them
dispatch themselves. It happens in their rooms
and books, in blankets, in their buried beds,
the bedrock of their basements, in their graves.
The rock, in presence or in absence, glows
like old love letters. It endures, no matter,
when no more dreams are stirring on the farm
and no true feeling leaves no memory.

INSULARITY:
OR, THE UNDOING OF ENGLAND

Browning and Yeats and Arnold, dreaming dreams
of teeming continents and emperors,
Canutes upon an island, castaways,
despised *La Manche* and yearned to walk on land.
> *How bare the rock, how desolate,*
> *Which had received our precious freight:*
> *Yet we call'd out—'Depart!*
> *Our gifts, once given, must here abide . . . '*
Thus Browning, with a woman on a litter,
rose and crossed over to the holy side.

Arnold, obedient son, acquainting himself
with the best that has been known and said in the world,
thrust Culture on his poor disorder'd island:
> *And in their glens, on starry nights,*
> *The nightingales divinely sing;*
> *And lovely notes, from shore to shore*
> *Across the sounds and channels pour . . .*

I hear it in the deep heart's core, Yeats crooned,
(a mossy place to hide a honeyed island,
a *deep heart* somehow heartened by a *core,*
more uterus than heart, a cuckoo clock
ticking inside.) What, *low sounds by the shore?*
The whirr of history's wings uplifted him
to travel naked, far beyond his island,
(*the salmon-falls, the mackerel-crowded seas*)
his Erin, eastward, emperor and canary—
but hammered gold and domes were all in vain.
And now we stare astonished at the sea,
and a miraculous strange bird shrieks at us.

57

The island, trailing clouds of weeds and cables,
dislodged its anchor and began to drift.
No longer stationary in the sea
it moved at will, not either land nor water,
a floating pasture, cattle munching corn
as ghosts of coral islands cast their shadow.
Like other forms of being it aspires
to an alliance with a higher form,
either with continents or with the sea.
So islands, married with a coral ring
or perched above a molten mountain's maw,
move west. Or wash away. Or disappear.

> *Oh then a longing like despair*
> *Is to their farthest caverns sent:*
> *For surely once, they feel, we were*
> *Parts of a single continent . . .*

Those islands won't stay anchored any longer,
no matter how many generations have called
them blesséd. Their coal, steel, steamships
supplied our cities, our satanic mills.
Here, stars apart, on unimagined shores
whose islands often stagger under cities,

> *(Lo, body and soul, this land,*
> *My own Manhattan, with spires, and the*
> *sparkling and hurrying tides . . .)*

we blink. Each citizen, an emperor,
clings like a postage stamp upon a cliff.
Below us, huge machines unearth the earth.
They gorge the burning cities of the plain
upon its flesh. Guts trail down from the belly.
The watercourses stain with coal and blood.

We have inherited a continent,
blue-black with stifled pride and guilt at what
we've eaten, importations from the islands,
beginning long ago with slaves and rum,
with silk, patchouli, immigrants and poets.
We plucked from islanders the fruit of empire,
learned at what cost the strong pay off their servants,
then filled our continent with islanders.
We sucked the teats of the land until it dried
and turned against our mother, angry
at being weaned. Our rivers were dammed up.
Cities were swollen till they smelled of death.
Death nudged the unfathomable sea.
A curse on the white-cliffed islands left behind—
a curse we have made good: the island's drifting.

XXI

Islands are honored still behind our shoulder.
Selected princely navigators set
their course against the currents, winds, and tides
to walk on islands that are truly desert,
unclothe the main lands with their reeking cities,
and worship, on the mountains of the moon,
blind faces squinting up toward the stars.

CREATURES OF THE GENITIVE

For Frances Lindley

*Adjectives of desire, knowledge,
memory, power, fullness, sharing,
and guilt take the genitive.*

RULE OF LATIN GRAMMAR

FULLNESS

Something lay hidden deep within the mountain.
I don't know what. Perhaps it could be love,
although I heard reports that thirsty tigers
had skulked around the heights in search of water
and startled tourists, full of food and wine,
exciting fear and other kinds of tension.

MEMORY

No wonder dreams like mine gave rise to tension
beyond whatever talk one heard of tigers.
What the high country left me with was love.
It followed me to settle near salt water,
but dreams went on for years beneath the mountain,
and memories as dizzying as wine.

GUILT

The palate seldom has enough of wine,
but excess of indulgence heightens tension
so that your thirst transcends the power of love
to slake, a guilt as terrible as tigers.
A hundred strolls around our homely mountain
in quest, in endless quest, of crystal water

SHARING

(O how dry country troubles you with water!)
brought me up short, or face to face with tigers
near brooks or lakes half up (or down) the mountain.
I tell you, I have had my share of tension.
Beneath the heights where all the world drinks wine,
two can afford the luxury of love.

DESIRE

One's second guess would have to be that love,
a thing as precious as untasted wine,
whether it wears the form of rocky mountains
or the transparent coverlet of tension,
is what the heart seeks when it desireth water.
But try to tell that to a thirsty tiger.

KNOWLEDGE

The hunger of the soul's a dream of tigers
mauling and snarling. Blunt their fangs with wine,
kiss knowledge in a whirlwind, crawl toward water,
trifle with fire and earthquake, piss on love,
lose nerve in each entanglement with tension—
and still a small voice murmurs in the mountain.

POWER

Though memory tenses with the guilt of tigers,
knowledge, desire, and love share sweetest water
when the strong mountain fills itself with wine.

PETER DAVISON

Born in New York in 1928, raised in Colorado
and educated at Harvard and Cambridge, Peter
Davison has been an editor in book publishing
houses since 1950. Since 1957 he has written poetry,
criticism of poetry, and autobiographical prose.
Peter Davison was the winner of the Yale Series of
Younger Poets Competition in 1964 and received an
award in literature from the National Institute of
Arts and Letters in 1972. He lives and works in Boston, where he is Director of the Atlantic Monthly
Press and poetry editor of *The Atlantic*. The ways by
which he arrived at a dual life are described in his
candid autobiographical book, *Half Remembered: A
Personal Hi.*

PS
3554
A94
V6

Davison, Peter.
    A voice in the mountain.

PS3554 A94 V6
+A voice in the m+Davison, Peter.

0 00 02 0208445 5
MIDDLEBURY COLLEGE

OEMCO

BY PETER DAVISON

POEMS

AUTOBIOGRAPHY